MARIJUANA

Sarah Lennard-Brown

R Raintree

Chicago, Illinois

Copyright Permissions
Raintree
100 N. LaSalle
Suite 1200
Chicago, IL 60602

Design: Carole Binding
Photo research: Glass Onion Pictures
Printed in China bound in the United States.

09 08 07 06 05
1 2 3 4 5 6 7 8 9 0

Library of Congress Cataloging-in-Publication Data:

Lennard-Brown, Sarah.
  Marijuana / Sarah Lennard-Brown.
    p. cm. -- (Health issues)
  Includes bibliographical references and index.
  Contents: The history of marijuana -- Taking marijuana -- The marijuana plant today -- Marijuana and the law.
  ISBN 0-7398-6896-9 (lib. bdg.)
  1. Marijuana--Juvenile literature. 2. Marijuana abuse--Juvenile literature. [1. Marijuana. 2. Drug abuse.] I. Title. II. Series.
  HV5822.M3L38 2005
  362.29'5--dc22
                                    2003026863

Acknowledgments

The author and publishers thank the following for their permission to reproduce photographs and illustrations: Cover and pp.1, 45, 58 Topham/PA; pp.4, 7 Science Photo Library (James King-Holmes); pp.9, 24 Rex Features (Sipa Press); p.10 Science Photo Library (Dave Reede/Agstock); p.13 Corbis (Roger Wood); pp.16, 19 Topham Picturepoint; p.17 Popperfoto; p.21 Corbis (Ted Streshinsky); p.23 Corbis (David Cumming; Eye Ubiquitous); pp.26, 43 Angela Hampton Family Life Picture Library; p.27 Corbis (Jennie Woodcock; Reflections Photolibrary); p.29 Rex Features (Bernadette Lou); pp.30, 38, 44 Topham/ImageWorks (©Esbin-Anderson); p.32 Science Photo Library (Faye Norman); p.34 Science Photo Library (Jim Varney); p.37 Corbis (James L. Amos); p.41 Science Photo Library (Simon Fraser/Royal Victoria Infirmary, Newcastle); p.47 Rex Features(David White); p.48 Rex Features (Ray Tang); p.51 Corbis (Stone Les/Corbis Sygma); p.53 Corbis (Roger Garwood and Trish Ainslie); p.54 Topham/ImageWorks (©Skjold); p.56 Corbis (Paul Hardy). The illustration on page 28 is by Carole Binding.

Note: Photographs illustrating the case studies in this book were posed by models.

Every effort has been made to trace copyright holders. However, the publishers apologize for any unintentional omissions and would be pleased in such cases to add an acknowledgment in any future editions.

Contents

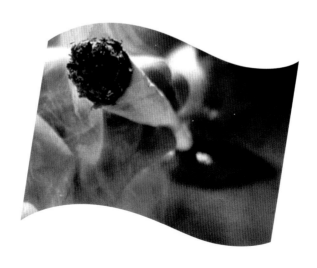

Introduction
A Drug with a Difference

The United Nations Office on Drugs and Crime estimates that, worldwide, 180 million people over the age of fifteen used drugs recreationally at some point during the late 1990s. This is about 4.2 percent of the world's population. Out of the total who had taken drugs, by far the largest group—144 million people—had taken marijuana.

What is cannabis? What is marijuana?

Cannabis is a plant that has been used in many ways for thousands of years. Its fibers have been used to make rope, paper, and cloth. Cannabis seeds have been food for people and animals. The plant has also been used to make medicines. In addition people discovered that smoking or eating some parts of the plant has an intoxicating effect. The drug marijuana is made from the dried leaves and flowering buds of the cannabis plant. Marijuana users say that it makes them feel relaxed, happy, and stimulated. This effect comes from chemicals that are present in the plant. They affect the user's brain and nervous system. There is more about the history of cannabis in chapter 1, and about its effects on the mind and body in chapter 2.

An amazing plant, a complex argument

The cannabis plant is useful in many ways, but its psychoactive qualities have given it a checkered past and an uncertain future.

Two types of cannabis plant

Over the centuries that people have used the cannabis plant, it has been selectively bred to improve its usefulness. Today there are two main varieties.

Cannabis sativa *plants are tall, growing up to 2 feet (6 meters) high, and can be planted very close together. They are also resistant to many common plant diseases. This means that cannabis sativa grows very well. The fibers produced by the plants are very long, which makes them suitable for spinning and weaving. The concentration of the chemicals that produce the intoxicating effect of marijuana is so low in cannabis sativa that this variety of the plant is not considered to be "psychoactive" (affecting the brain and producing intoxication). Cannabis sativa tends to be grown by people wishing to use the plant in industrial processes.*

Cannabis indica *is a small shrubby plant, which produces a high concentration of the chemicals that produce intoxication. People wishing to use the plant as an intoxicant usually grow cannabis indica.*

A controversial drug

For most drugs that people take recreationally there is no dispute about the damage they do to the user and to society. For example, few people argue that crack cocaine is not addictive and that people should be free to use it. Crack cocaine is so addictive that users often resort to crime to obtain money to buy the drugs they crave. The drug itself can make users violent. However, in the case of marijuana, there is much debate. Some people argue that marijuana is less harmful than tobacco and alcohol, and does not cause users to become violent or so addicted that they commit crimes to obtain money to buy the drug. They feel that the law should be changed so that adults can use marijuana if they wish. A different point of view is that marijuana is a "gateway drug," introducing people to the world of illegal drugs and leading them on to abuse drugs that are more harmful. People who see marijuana in this way argue that it should remain an illegal drug.

The plant's intoxicating chemicals

The highest concentration of intoxicating chemicals is found in the resin of the cannabis plant. The resin is produced to protect the flowers from the heat of the sun and to help trap pollen grains to fertilize the plant. The leaves and stalk also contain intoxicating chemicals. The growing conditions of the plant (for example, how sunny it is) and how it is harvested, stored, and processed all affect the amount of intoxicant there is in the final drug.

How marijuana is sold

Marijuana is sold in a variety of forms:

- Dried leaves contain a fairly low level of the plant's intoxicating chemicals.
- Fertilized flowering tops usually contain a medium amount of intoxicant.
- Unfertilized flowering tops, sometimes called sinsemilla (which means "without seeds"), contain a higher concentration of intoxicant.

The above three forms of marijuana are the forms most commonly available in the United States and are sometimes known as pot, grass, weed, reefer, herb, and ganga.

- Cannabis resin is produced by separating it from the flowering buds, and is usually sold as a dark brown lump, solid and slightly oily. The amount of intoxicant in resin varies, depending on the amount of plant material in it. Resin is more common in Britain and Western Europe. Common names for it include hashish, hash, bhang, charas, black, and brown.
- Hash oil is produced by boiling the cannabis plant in alcohol, filtering out the plant solids, and letting the remaining liquid evaporate. The oil contains an even higher concentration of intoxicant than resin.

"Cannabis resin looks like a brownish ball of gunk, often very small if it's for personal use."
(Ahmed, police officer)

How cannabis drugs are taken

Cannabis preparations are either inhaled or eaten. In the Western world, marijuana is most commonly smoked in the form of a "joint." Joints are usually constructed by rolling the dried plant or resin in a homemade cigarette. Other ways of inhaling marijuana include smoking it in a tobacco pipe or using an apparatus called a "bong" (a large pipe). Occasionally, a piece of resin is heated under a glass and the fumes are inhaled.

"I can always tell if my brother's been smoking pot. There's a sort of green smell like hay and a strong smell of incense that he burns to try to cover it up."
(Amy, age 15)

Sometimes cannabis preparations are added to food, such as cookies or cakes, and eaten. These foods can be dangerous to people who eat them unknowingly. Children have ended up in the hospital, unconscious, from unwittingly eating "pot brownies."

Different forms
The different forms of the cannabis drug include cannabis resin or hash (in the foreground) and dried leaves and flowering tops.

Common names for cannabis

Marijuana	Black
Hashish	Gold
Pot	Hash oil
Hash	Smoke
Grass	Spliff
Reefer	Herb
Ganja	Dope
Weed	Mary Jane
Tar	Bhang

Where marijuana is grown

In the mid-20th century, many countries passed laws designed to stop people from using harmful recreational drugs. These included laws prohibiting the growing of marijuana. As a result, the number of countries producing illegal drug crops has come down. However, during the 1990s, 130 countries still reported illegal cultivation of marijuana to the United Nations Office on Drugs and Crime.

Marijuana grows better in some climates than others. *Cannabis indica* grown in bright sunlight produces the highest concentration of intoxicating chemicals. Some of the strongest preparations of the drug are produced by growing the plant indoors, under controlled conditions. However, this method of growing is very expensive and so most illegal marijuana is grown where the climate is most suitable. The greatest amount of illegal marijuana is grown in South America and Asia.

United Nations

The United Nations Office on Drugs and Crime was set up in 1997 to coordinate the international fight against drugs and crime. It collects information about drug production, drug smuggling, and drug use around the world. It advises governments about making laws to combat drug abuse in their countries. It is also involved in investigating and prosecuting drug-related crime and terrorism.

The marijuana trade

From the places where it is produced, marijuana is smuggled into countries around the world. This trade is illegal and customs officers and police try to stop it. Most of the marijuana seizures they make occur in just a few countries: Columbia, India, Mexico, Morocco, the Netherlands, Pakistan, South Africa, Spain, the United Kingdom, and the United States. Marijuana accounts for the largest amount of illegal drug traffic around the world.

Marijuana laws today

Ever since marijuana was made illegal, some people have argued that the laws should be changed. In trying to stop marijuana from being used as a recreational drug, the lawmakers had also prevented the cannabis plant from being used in the manufacture of several useful products. Some people say that marijuana is a helpful medicine for treating or relieving the symptoms of some serious illnesses. These arguments, as well as the argument that marijuana as a recreational drug is not harmful, have been put forward by people who campaign for marijuana use to be legalized.

Over time some countries have relaxed their laws on marijuana, and these laws have become a "hot" political issue. Chapter 3 looks at the potential uses of the cannabis plant in today's world, and chapter 4 investigates how different countries try to control the use of marijuana among their population. It also presents the arguments that people put forward on both sides.

Marijuana and you

With laws on marijuana being a popular topic for discussion, it is likely that you already have some ideas about the drug. You may know people who have used the drug or are regular users. You may have been invited to try marijuana yourself, or this may happen fairly soon. The purpose of this book is to give you the information you need to make up your own mind about the issue and to make the healthiest choice for yourself.

Being there
It can be fun being part of the scene and hanging out with friends, but it must always be your own decision when it comes to taking substances that could affect your health.

1 The History of Cannabis
A Plant with Many Uses

The cannabis plant probably originated in central Asia, where the ancient nomads found its tough, fibrous stems so useful that they took its seeds with them when they moved around. Traces of cannabis plants have been found as far apart as in the tombs of the ancient Egyptians and in China, where cannabis has been grown as a crop since people started to settle in that part of the world. One of the earliest records of people using the cannabis plant has been found in Taiwan, an island close to China. Archaeologists found a clay pot that had been decorated with cord made from cannabis fibers. This Stone Age pot was made over 10,000 years ago.

The ancient Chinese

The ancient Chinese found that fibers twisted together were stronger than single fibers and so they started to produce rope. The strong, long fibers they needed came from the cannabis plant. They also began to weave the fibers together to produce cloth. China is famous for its silk. Silk is woven from the fine threads produced by silkworms, but these are very expensive and so silk could only be afforded by the rich. Cannabis fibers (called hemp) were far cheaper to

Useful history
The long stems of cannabis have been used since earliest times for their fiber.

produce and cannabis became such an important crop that the ancient Chinese referred to their country as "the land of mulberry and hemp" (silkworms feed on mulberry leaves).

The Chinese realized that the cannabis plant had multiple uses. They discovered that the male plants produced better fiber for rope and cloth, and the female plants produced seeds, which were a nutritious food for animals and people. The Chinese found that the strength and flexibility of hemp fibers made them suitable for producing high-quality bowstrings for their archers. These bowstrings were so important in maintaining China's military superiority that large areas were set aside to grow hemp exclusively for this use.

One of China's many great innovations was the invention of paper. Before paper the Chinese wrote on slips of wood, which were very heavy. Silk was used occasionally for special documents, but this was very expensive. The first evidence of paper dates back to the first century B.C.E. Hemp was the main fiber in paper and continued to be used across the world for nearly 2,000 years. The first drafts of the American Declaration of Independence, in 1776, were written on hemp paper.

Paper

The Chinese first made paper by soaking ground-up mulberry tree bark and hemp fibers in a tank of water. The fibers were then skimmed from the top of the tank in molds and left to dry. The Chinese closely guarded the secret of making paper. The first people to discover this secret were Arabs, and they started Europe's first paper mill in 1150.

The ancient Chinese also investigated the medical properties of marijuana. From at least as long ago as the 28th century B.C.E., they used marijuana preparations to treat menstrual problems, rheumatism, constipation, gout, and many other conditions. It was also used as a pain reliever. Later the intoxicating effects of marijuana were used in religious settings to help people "communicate with the spirits."

Japan and India

Cannabis production is woven through the history of many great civilizations, including Japan and India. In Japan, like China, cannabis was valued for its fiber and commonly used in the production of cloth. It also became an essential component of medicines and religious ceremonies.

In India one of the Hindu gods, Shiva, is said to have brought the cannabis plant down from the Himalayan mountains for "use and enjoyment." The earliest written reference to the psychoactive (mind-changing) properties of cannabis is found in an ancient Hindu text, called the *Atharva-veda*, which is thought to date from approximately 2000 B.C.E. Unlike in the Far East, marijuana became popular as an intoxicant and was often prepared as a concoction, mixed with other herbs and spices, and used in a similar way to alcohol in the West. Different varieties of the concoction were called bhang, charas, and ganja, and were used to celebrate weddings and births, as symbols of hospitality and welcome, to fortify soldiers in battle, and to aid communication with the gods in religious ceremonies. Cannabis was also used as a food (hemp seeds) and as a medicine to treat dysentery, sunstroke, and digestive disorders.

The Buddha

According to the Mahayana Buddhist tradition, the Buddha is supposed to have survived on one hemp seed a day during a long fast.

Ancient Greeks and Romans

The ancient Greeks recognized the many uses of the cannabis plant. It is referred to in *The Histories* written by Herodotus (c. 485–425 B.C.E.). The Greeks did not use the plant for its intoxicating properties, but valued it as a source of fiber. In the 6th century B.C.E., the Greeks were carrying on a thriving trade in hemp fiber. They also used the seeds as a treatment for backache and as a food.

Hemp rope was very important for the Roman Empire, especially to equip Roman ships, and large quantities of cannabis were imported, mainly from Babylon. The Romans also recognized the medicinal uses of marijuana, and marijuana is mentioned in the first

Western directory of healing plants, *Materia medica*, written by Dioscorides in 70 C.E. The famous Roman doctor Galen (130–200 C.E.) wrote about marijuana as a cure for earache and gout, but he noted that it could cause impotence in men who overindulged in it.

Europe and America

Europe was persuaded of the value of hemp rope and fiber. In 1563 Queen Elizabeth I of England passed laws that required owners of farms above a certain size to grow cannabis. The crop was so important, especially for rope for ships, that some English towns (Hemel Hempstead, for example) were named after it.

Cannabis was introduced to the North American continent by Spanish sailors in 1545, and it became an essential crop for the New World. In 1619 a law was passed at Jamestown Colony in Virginia requiring all farmers to grow cannabis for fiber.

Roman rope
The rope used on ancient Roman ships was made from hemp fibers.

"We still use hemp rope today. We use it on our sailing boat. It's very strong."
(Ben, sailor)

Cannabis Timeline

B.C.E.

10,000	Cannabis cord used to decorate a Stone Age pot in Taiwan.
8000–7000	Earliest evidence of cannabis fiber cloth, in China.
2700	Cannabis listed in the pharmacopoeia (list of medicinal plants) of Shen Nung (China).
2000	Psychoactive properties of cannabis mentioned in the ancient Hindu text, the **Atharva-veda.**
550	Cannabis listed in the **Zend-Avista,** a pharmacopoeia written by Zoroaster, a Persian prophet whose followers are credited with introducing the plant to India.
5th century	Greek historian Herodotus records the use of cannabis in **The Histories.**

C.E.

0–100	Chinese start making paper from hemp fiber.
70	**Materia medica**, a pharmacopoeia by Dioscorides, includes cannabis.
500–600	Greeks organize a profitable international trade in hemp fiber.
1150	First European paper mill using hemp fiber is built by Arabs at Xativa, in Spain.
1545	Cannabis is introduced to North America.
1563	Queen Elizabeth I of England orders landowners to grow cannabis.
1564	King Philip of Spain orders cannabis to be grown throughout his empire (from Argentina to Oregon).
1619	Legislation in Jamestown Colony, Virginia, orders farmers to grow cannabis for hemp production.
1776	First two drafts of the American Declaration of Independence are written on hemp paper. Betsy Ross sews the first U.S. flag, using hemp cloth.
1798	French Emperor Napoleon and his army invade Egypt, where they learn about smoking cannabis as a drug. When they return to France in 1801, they take the practice back with them.
1840	Club des Hachischins is established by bohemians in Paris.
1890	Queen Victoria's doctor, Sir Russell Reynolds, writes of prescribing marijuana for menstrual cramps.

1924	Second International Opiates Conference includes cannabis in a list of dangerous drugs whose production and use should be reduced.
1925	Dangerous Drugs Act in the United Kingdom makes it illegal to import, export, process, produce, sell, or buy any drug on a list that includes heroin, cocaine, and marijuana.
1931	Marijuana Tax Act in the United States effectively stops the production of hemp fiber.
1941	Henry Ford creates a hemp car, made from and powered by cannabis.
1942	Restrictions on growing cannabis are lifted across the United States in order to supply the need for fiber during World War II.
1951	Narcotics Control Act in the United States introduces heavy penalties for possession of any cannabis product.
1961	United Nations Treaty 406 Single Convention on Narcotic Drugs: 40 countries agree to work toward eradicating the production and consumption of opium, cocaine, and marijuana.
1974	The Netherlands relaxes its drug laws to allow the sale of small amounts of marijuana, which must be used at regulated premises.
2000	Hawaii passes legislation to enable marijuana to be prescribed as a medicine for certain life-threatening illnesses. Hawaii is one of ten states that allow the use of marijuana as a medicine in some situations.

Discovering the drug

By the 1800s cannabis fiber was used all over the world to make rope, but the plant's intoxicating effects were not known in Europe. This situation changed after the French emperor Napoleon invaded Egypt in 1798. Napoleon's soldiers learned about cannabis as a drug from the Egyptians and took the discovery home to France. Nineteenth-century European scientists then investigated the new drug and this led to its becoming a popular remedy for many ailments. Sir Russell Reynolds, the medical advisor to Queen Victoria (1819–1901), prescribed the plant for insomnia (inability to sleep), nausea (feeling sick), and menstrual cramps. It was possible to buy cannabis preparations in pharmacies without a prescription until the 1890s.

Club des Hachischins

The Club des Hachischins was started in France in 1840 by a group of intellectuals, artists, and writers who met to talk and experiment with marijuana. The idea was that marijuana helped to stimulate their artistic and intellectual thinking. Members included the poets Charles Baudelaire and Arthur Rimbaud and the poet, novelist, and painter Pierre Gautier. This group was part of a larger group known as bohemians, who congregated in the cafés around Montmartre in Paris. They rebelled against the social conventions of their time, and held radical views on morality, art, and politics. Famous bohemians include the writer Victor Hugo and artists Jean-François Millet and Gustave Courbet.

Paris scene
Cafés in Paris became the center of the "Bohemian" movement in the second half of the 19th century.

Cannabis cultivation in the 20th century

The amount of cannabis grown across Europe and the United States decreased at the end of the 19th century and the beginning of the 20th century. Other crops were used for animal feeds, and new synthetic (humanmade) fibers were beginning to become available, replacing hemp. However, during World Wars I and II, the need to grow cannabis increased, in order to produce hemp fiber for making rope, sacking, and cloth. During World War II, in Britain, the United States, Canada, Australia, France, and particularly in Germany, growing cannabis was seen as a way of supporting the national war effort. Before, these countries had been getting the hemp they needed from Russia, but the supply was now cut off because Russia was at war with Germany. To meet their increased need for hemp fiber, each country vastly increased its cultivation of cannabis. In 1943 the United States issued a "pro hemp" propaganda film called *Hemp for Victory,* in which farmers were shown how best to cultivate the crop and the many uses to which it could be put. However, as soon as the war was over, this policy was revoked.

War effort
Growing hemp was encouraged during World War II. One important use of the fiber was to make sacking for sandbags.

Marijuana becomes an illegal drug

As cannabis ceased to be so important as a crop, there began to be increasing publicity about the intoxicating effects of marijuana, and there were calls for laws to prevent people from using it. During the late 19th and early 20th centuries, concern grew about the effects of intoxicating substances on the general population. In Great Britain there were worries about the number of people abusing laudanum (a form of opium that could be purchased without prescription) and also alcohol. In the United States there was increasing concern about the effects of all intoxicating substances. These substances were seen as the cause of many social problems and it was felt that people needed to be protected from their evil influence.

Several international conferences were held to investigate the effect of intoxicating substances on the general population. In 1924, the Second International Opiates Conference at the Hague in the Netherlands looked not only at opiates (drugs such as heroin and morphine, produced from the sap of the opium poppy) but at all intoxicating drugs. The conference produced an agreement to control and reduce the production and use of narcotic drugs across the world, and marijuana was included in the list.

This was the beginning of a worldwide campaign against recreational drugs. There was an era of prohibition around the world, during which it was illegal to produce, sell, or buy intoxicating drugs (including alcohol in the United States). However, making a substance illegal does not stop people from wanting to take it or from being addicted to it. Drug production and supply became a profitable secret occupation for criminals and smugglers.

Violent connection?

During the 1920s and 1930s newspapers portrayed marijuana as causing violent behavior. Research into marijuana and violence has not found any connection between the two.

Prohibition

During Prohibition (1920–1933), it was illegal to produce, sell, or buy intoxicating drugs, including alcohol. People found ways of hiding alcohol to use in secret. Some people argue that laws to discourage the use of drugs actually make them more attractive and increase their use.

The anti-drug movement was taken up enthusiastically by newspaper editors and several influential people in the United States, including a man named Henry Anslinger who became head of the Federal Bureau of Narcotics in 1930. He started a campaign against all drugs, in particular marijuana, which he felt made people violent and lazy. There were protests from the hemp industry, who saw their livelihood being made illegal, and from some doctors, who felt that the reasons given for criminalizing cannabis were unfounded. Nevertheless, in 1937 the Marijuana Tax Law was passed. It stated that anyone selling cannabis (whether for use as a drug or as fiber) had to pay a "transfer tax." Under this law, you could only apply for a "tax stamp" when you were in possession of cannabis, but being in possession of cannabis without having paid the stamp was illegal. This meant that it was impossible to be legally in possession of cannabis, and so the Tax Law effectively made the production of hemp fiber illegal.

Further laws in the United States, including the Narcotics Control Act of 1951, introduced heavy fines for people found in possession of, selling, or smuggling cannabis, whether it was for use as a drug or as a fiber. This eliminated the production of what had once been an important crop across the country. By 1950, farming of cannabis was banned across the entire United States.

Henry Ford and the chemurgical movement

One of the people who thought that cannabis was useful was the industrialist Henry Ford. He was a supporter of the Farm Chemurgic Council, which was formed in 1935 by people who believed that the normal crops grown by farmers could be used to develop unlimited new products and technologies. At this time, the developments of the petrochemical industry (producing plastics, nylons, dyes and paints, etc.) were in their infancy. Supporters of the chemurgical movement argued that all these products could be produced just as well from plants as from petroleum, and that plants had the added advantage that they would not dry up like oil wells.

In 1941 Henry Ford was investigating how crops could be converted into fuels and materials for the automobile industry. He was very excited by the use of ethyl alcohol, made from fermented hemp and other vegetation, as a fuel. He felt this would be ideal to power machinery, including his new cars. He also produced a prototype car with a strong and robust body made from hemp fiber strengthened with resin. But, unfortunately for Henry Ford, the tide of opinion against all forms of cannabis meant that his plans for the car had to be abandoned. Today, companies such as Mercedes Benz and Daimler use a lot of hemp fiber in their factories and there are plans to use hemp fiber and resin in car bodies, just as Henry Ford suggested in 1941.

A symbol of rebellion

With hindsight, it can be seen that making marijuana illegal did little to reduce its use as an intoxicant. Some people argue that the laws actually encouraged more people to try the drug, as it became a symbol around which rebellious groups could rally. The first group to use marijuana in this way were the "beat generation." This group, who are identified with Jack Kerouac, Allen Ginsberg, and Ken Kesey, rebelled against the social conventions of the 1950s and sought freedom and self-expression. In part, this meant that they were promiscuous and took a lot of drugs. However, their idea of exploring your own mind and realizing your artistic potential with the aid of illegal narcotics (including marijuana) created a sense of romance and excitement. This was very exciting for a generation of young people who had been brought up during the hardships of World War II.

Merry Pranksters

The writer Ken Kesey (1935–2001) was a leading figure in American counter-culture, known for using marijuana and other drugs. His followers became known as the Merry Pranksters and in the 1960s they made a famous journey from San Francisco to New York in his "Magic Bus," painted in psychedelic colors.

The 1960s and into the present

Marijuana use as a drug really became popular during the 1960s. It began to be part of the popular youth scene. The "Summer of Love" in 1967 saw a surge in the use of marijuana as an intoxicant in the Western world. Several movie and music stars were arrested for possession of marijuana.

Marijuana was also closely associated with the Caribbean island of Jamaica and with the Rastafarian religion, which became popular there during the 1930s. Marijuana was probably introduced to the island by Indian laborers in the 1800s. The common Jamaican name for it is "ganja," which comes from India. Marijuana is used by Rastafarians as part of their religious ritual and as a medicine. Rastafarians feel that the Jamaican laws that prevent them from using marijuana in their religious rituals are wrong. They continue to fight to be allowed to use it.

"In 1967 we were so full of hope for a new world. There was lots of talk about drugs, but I never took any. I didn't really see any. I wouldn't have known what to do with them. I think there is more pot around today than there was then."
(Marion, age 57)

The Rastafarian religion

Rastafarianism is a religion and a way of life. Its religious book is the Bible, but Rastafarians interpret it differently from most Christian religions. They see white political power as "Babylon," an evil oppressive power that keeps Rastas in bondage. One of the prime beliefs of the Rastafarian religion is that Emperor Haile Selassie I of Ethiopia was a god. The name Rastafarian comes from Haile Selassie's original name, Tafari, preceded by "Ras," meaning "prince." When Haile Selassie was murdered in 1975, many Rastafarians refused to believe that he was dead. They now believe that he "Sits on the highest point of Mount Zion," awaiting the time of judgment. Selassie was a Christian and did not view himself as a god.

Rastafarians consider Africa to be "heaven on earth." They believe that Jah (God) will send a signal and that they will travel back to Ethiopia. This is called the "exodus," like the Bible story of the Israelites escaping from slavery in Egypt and entering the "promised land."

Rastafarians
One distinctive feature of Rastafarians is that they wear their hair in long dreadlocks. Marijuana is used as part of some Rastafarian religious ceremonies.

As the 20th century progressed, marijuana and hemp were the subject of much debate. Individuals and groups fought to be allowed to use it as a medicine and as an industrial material, and some people argued that the law should be changed so that marijuana could be used as a recreational drug. In chapter 3 we will look at how marijuana and hemp are used in today's world, but first we will explore the effects that marijuana has on people who use it recreationally.

2 Taking Marijuana
The Effects on Mind and Body

People who take marijuana recreationally say that it makes them relaxed and happy. They feel a mix of peacefulness, hilarity, and drowsiness. In general, people who smoke marijuana feel stimulated and happy at first. These feelings are followed about half an hour later by drowsiness.

Marijuana is unique in that it seems that the brain may have to learn how to respond to it. The first time some people use marijuana, they hardly notice any effects. If they use it again, the effects become more noticeable.

How the intoxicants enter the body

When a person smokes marijuana, hundreds of chemicals in the smoke are quickly absorbed by his or her lungs. Within minutes the chemicals enter the bloodstream and are taken to the heart, brain, and other organs. The most psychoactive chemical in marijuana smoke (the one that affects the brain the most) is called delta-9-tetrahydrocannabinol—THC for short. The huge number of chemicals contained in marijuana have not been fully researched, and so it is still unclear whether they react with each other to produce the effects and how exactly they cause the effects. Most research has concentrated on the effects of THC.

Taking in THC
Marijuana smoke contains the psychoactive substance THC, or delta-9-tetrahydrocannabinol. It quickly passes via the user's lungs into the bloodstream.

Most of the THC that reaches the brain is broken down and removed by the body's natural mechanisms within a few hours. However, other organs, such as the kidneys, liver, spleen, and testes, do not get rid of THC as fast. In the liver some of the THC is converted into compounds that stay around for several days. Some of these compounds also have psychoactive effects, so, although the first effects of marijuana are over within a few hours, the drug continues to be present in the bloodstream and to affect the brain and body for several days.

THC is taken up by body fat, which acts as an energy store for the body when there is not enough food to meet its energy needs. When the body fat is broken down to release the energy, the THC is also released into the bloodstream again. So, even if someone has not smoked marijuana for several weeks, it may still be detectable in his or her body and may still affect the person.

Immediate effects

The effects of smoking marijuana vary, depending on the concentration of intoxicating chemicals it contains. When high-grade marijuana is used, the effects are felt less quickly, but when they do occur, they can be almost hallucinogenic (causing the person to see, feel, smell, or hear something that does not exist). The person may experience a heightened awareness of colors or smells and of his or her body. The user may be very aware of his or her heart pumping and the blood flowing around the veins, or of muscles tensing and relaxing. This can be frightening and cause the person to panic. Someone may go to the hospital because he or she is afraid. However, the best treatment is quiet, calm reassurance. The sensation will eventually diminish.

Low-grade marijuana has very little effect. Sometimes it is referred to as "headache pot," because the user tends to get a feeling of heaviness in their head or a headache, rather than a "high."

Eating marijuana

When marijuana is eaten, larger amounts tend to be taken, and so the effect lasts for longer and can be more intense.

The effects of marijuana depend on the individual. Many people do not experience anything the first, or even the first few times they take the drug. How experienced users feel when they use marijuana also varies. Some feel that they understand the world better; others feel happy. The feeling people get when they use the drug often depends on the environment they are in and the people they are with. Sometimes the experience is not pleasant.

The effects of taking marijuana on the body are easier to identify. The user's eyes become bloodshot and his or her face may become flushed red. The user may feel his or her heart beating more quickly. Smoking marijuana also produces an effect called "the munchies"—an intense feeling of hunger that is difficult to satisfy.

People often have difficulty recalling what it was like when they took the drug, and this may be due to its effect on memory. Smoking marijuana disrupts the ability to remember things. Users often report that time seems to slow down when they smoke pot: A few

I'm worried about my brother

"My brother smokes pot occasionally. I don't think my parents notice, but I do. His eyes get all red and he eats everything in the house. He says he does it because his friends do it. I think he's pathetic. I don't think the pot has much effect on him really, he always sleeps a lot anyway. I haven't told anyone. I'm worried what Mom and Dad will say if he gets caught. Someone told me that, if the police catch him with pot here, my parents will be in trouble, too. He just laughs and says no one is going to catch him. I don't know what to do. All he thinks about is himself."

(Andrew, age 15)

minutes can seem to take forever. This may also be due to the effect of marijuana on memory and concentration. These feelings can last at least 48 hours after taking the drug and can recur up to three weeks later, as the last traces of THC are removed from the body.

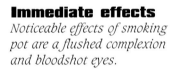

Immediate effects

Noticeable effects of smoking pot are a flushed complexion and bloodshot eyes.

Short-term and long-term effects of marijuana

Short-term effects	Long-term effects
Relaxation	Memory formation and learning are impaired for 48 hours or more.
Sedation	
Hilarity	Functioning of immune system is probably affected.
Tranquillity	
Lack of aggression	Lung disease (probably related to smoke inhalation).
Impaired judgment	
Increased heart rate	High doses can result in decreased sperm count for males and irregular periods for women.
Flushing	
Blood-shot eyes	
Inhibition of memory	Brain development of unborn child can be affected if marijuana is smoked during pregnancy.
Inhibition of ability to learn	
Hunger ("munchies")	

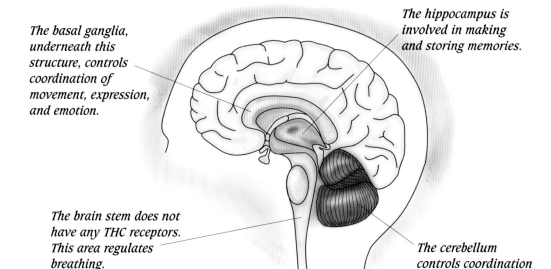

The basal ganglia, underneath this structure, controls coordination of movement, expression, and emotion.

The hippocampus is involved in making and storing memories.

The brain stem does not have any THC receptors. This area regulates breathing.

The cerebellum controls coordination of movement.

Marijuana and the brain

One fascinating thing about marijuana is that there appear to be specific structures in the human brain that recognize and respond to THC. They have been called the cannabinoid receptors, and they are found in several areas of the brain, including the hippocampus, the cerebellum, and the basal ganglia. There are no receptors for THC in the brain stem, an area that controls breathing. The lack of THC receptors in this area may explain why an overdose of marijuana is not fatal.

Marijuana is not the only plant for which there are specific brain receptors. Our brains also have opiate receptors, which respond to opiate drugs such as heroin and morphine. It is known that our opiate receptors exist because we naturally produce a chemical similar to opiates, called an endorphin, to regulate pain and stress within our bodies. Therefore, it would be logical to think that, since our brains have THC receptors, we must also naturally produce a chemical that is similar to THC.

There are two main neurotransmitters (chemicals) in the brain that stimulate the cannabinoid (THC) receptors. They are anandamide and 2-AG. What these neurotransmitters do and how they work is not yet

The brain

There are cannabinoid receptors in the areas of our brain known as the basal ganglia, the hippocampus, and the cerebellum. Each area controls different functions.

completely understood, but it would seem that anandamide has something to do with feelings of tranquillity and 2-AG decreases the ability of the brain to use memories efficiently. Why the brain produces a chemical that reduces the ability to remember is not clear. It may be to restrict the ability to remember things that are very painful or damaging. These effects of anandamide and 2-AG can both be observed when people use marijuana.

In fact, the effects of marijuana on memory and the ability to create new memories mean that taking the drug can result in poor performance at school, work, or play.

"My friend Glen dropped out of college. His teachers said he wasn't trying hard enough, but really it was drugs. He got in with a group of guys who smoked a lot. He got all laid back and just didn't care about anything.'"
(Mark, age 20)

Some of the cannabinoid receptors are in the cerebellum and basal ganglia. These parts of the brain are involved in the coordination of movement and the judgment required in making fine movements.

Marijuana is similar to alcohol in the way it disrupts the user's ability to control movement, making it dangerous to drive or operate machinery when a person uses the drug.

Keeping alert
To cycle safely in traffic, you need to be in control of your movement, well coordinated, and alert to everything that is happening around you. Marijuana has a negative effect on all those factors.

The majority of our THC receptors seem to be located in the hippocampus. This part of the brain is involved in making and storing memories. If your hippocampus is damaged, you have problems learning new tasks, but you can remember things you learned in the past.

Scientists researching the effects of THC have shown that, when rats are given THC, activity in the hippocampus is reduced. It returns to normal as the THC wears off. Other rat and primate experiments have shown that, under normal conditions, THC does not seem to produce long-term damage to the structure of brain cells. Only if the doses are much higher than a human would normally be able to take does some damage to brain cells occur.

Some scientists are cautious about this. They feel that THC may change the way brain cells connect with each other, or may change the concentrations of the chemicals in the brain that enable brain cells to communicate. These sorts of changes are very hard to show when a brain is examined under a microscope. However, some studies of people who have used marijuana for many years have shown that there may be difficulties with memory and problem-solving. This needs further study to be sure that the difficulties are not due to THC present in the individuals at the time of the test, rather than being due to long-term, heavy marijuana use.

Heart rate

Marijuana makes the user's heart beat much faster than normal. The feeling is the same as when you get very strenuous exercise.

Marijuana and the heart

Marijuana has the effect of increasing the user's heartbeat. A user may feel his or her heart is racing, as it would after running or when very excited or nervous. The increase in the heart rate can be as much as 20 to 30 beats per minute. An average adult has a heart rate of 60 to 70 beats per minute, so raising this to 90 or 100 beats per minute is a big raise. However, it is quite normal for the heart rate to rise to as much as 120 or 130 beats per minute during strenuous exercise, with no bad effects on the person's health. So, it would seem that the kind of rise in heart rate caused by marijuana would not be dangerous for someone in good health, with an average normal heart rate. It could be dangerous for someone whose heart rate is already higher than average, due to high blood pressure or heart disease.

"My uncle has smoked pot for years. He tells everyone that it doesn't do him any harm, but he's got a cough like he smokes 40 cigarettes a day."
(Cassie, age 15)

Marijuana and the lungs

Smoking pot does affect the lungs. Often the damage caused by smoking pot is worse than that caused by smoking cigarettes. This is due to several factors. First, people smoking pot roll their own cigarettes. Unlike many manufactured cigarettes, these do not have filters, which help to reduce the amount of tar and chemicals that the smoker inhales. Second, to make sure that the maximum amount of the drug enters their system, marijuana users tend to take bigger breaths of smoke deep into their lungs and hold it there for longer than people who smoke cigarettes. This magnifies the damaging effects.

Tobacco smoke and marijuana smoke contain similar chemicals that damage the cells lining the lungs. Therefore people who smoke marijuana are at a risk similar to those who smoke a mixture of marijuana and tobacco. Lung, throat, and mouth cancers are known to be a risk for people who smoke tobacco. It is not known whether smoking marijuana can cause these cancers, but anyone smoking marijuana mixed with tobacco is clearly at risk.

Asthma

Marijuana can trigger an asthma attack for some people with asthma. They need to avoid smoking pot and to stay away from places where pot is smoked.

Marijuana and the immune system

There are THC receptors all over the body, not just in the brain. Some are found in the cells that control your immune system, by which your body protects itself from infectious illness and disease. Few studies have looked at this area. They show that marijuana may decrease the body's ability to fight infections. More research needs to be done before we can be sure.

Marijuana and the reproductive system

Using marijuana seems to affect the hormones that regulate sperm production in men and egg production in women. It does this by increasing the production of a hormone called prolactin. Two other effects of this on men may be difficulty in achieving and maintaining an erection and the growth of breast tissue. In women, the hormone disruption can result in irregular periods.

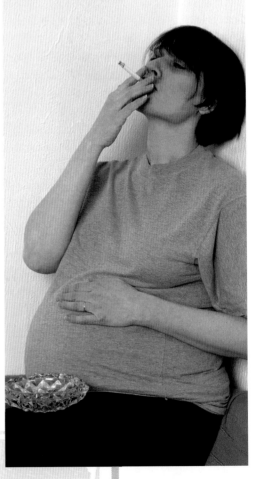

Smoking marijuana during pregnancy

Several studies have shown that babies born to women who used marijuana during pregnancy tend to weigh slightly less than other babies. In a study by Italian scientists in 2003, pregnant rats were injected with marijuana extracts. The baby rats that were born were found to be more "hyper" than normal and scored lower on learning tests throughout their lives. The scientists feel that this proves that marijuana can pass to the unborn child from the mother. Their work supports other studies showing that children born to mothers who smoked marijuana while pregnant may have long-term memory and learning problems.

Smoking risks

Smoking tobacco while pregnant carries risks to the unborn baby. Mixing marijuana with the tobacco adds further dangers.

Marijuana and mental health

The effect of marijuana on mental health is debated. Some people think there are links between marijuana use and depression and between marijuana use and schizophrenia, a disease of the mind that involves thought disturbance, unusual behavior, and loss of understanding of reality. Percentages of marijuana users with depression and schizophrenia are greater than the percentages of non-users with these disorders. However, this does not necessarily mean that marijuana causes the disorders. It could be that lifestyle, genetics, and family influences make people with depression and schizophrenia more likely to have the opportunity to use marijuana and more likely to become dependent on it.

"People who smoke pot ought to be aware that it has effects equal to those of cigarettes on the body, and worse effects on the mind."
(Dr. John Henry)

Although marijuana use has increased over the last half century, the proportion of marijuana users who have mental health problems has not increased. Some mental health researchers feel that people with certain mental health problems may use marijuana, like alcohol, in a mistaken attempt to control their problems. Other people think that, in order to develop mental health problems, a person must have a genetic tendency to them, and that marijuana may act as a switch, turning on an underlying problem. Clearly this area needs much more research.

"My brother smoked a lot of pot and then later we found out he had schizophrenia. I don't think the drugs caused it. I think he was just trying to make himself feel better by smoking pot."
(Miles, age 14)

Withdrawal from marijuana

With some recreational drugs, users experience unpleasant withdrawal symptoms when the drug is no longer in their body. They feel that they must keep taking the drug in order to avoid the withdrawal symptoms. In this way, they become physically dependent on, or addicted to, the drug. The withdrawal symptoms make the drug very hard to give up. By contrast, for low-level, short-term users of marijuana, there are no physical effects when they stop taking it. Withdrawing from heavy, long-term marijuana use can cause discomfort, but this is short-lived. Some reports suggest that long-term users can have problems sleeping when they stop taking the drug. They may feel restless, irritable, and anxious. With support, encouragement, and time these symptoms will eventually disappear.

It might seem that it would be easy to stop taking marijuana. However, psychological dependence can be very powerful. The person may feel that he or she cannot get through normal daily life without marijuana, and therefore it is very hard to stop. People who are psychologically dependent on marijuana may need support from professionals to help them find ways of relaxing or coping without the drug.

Talking down
An overdose of marijuana can cause extreme anxiety. The way to help a person in this situation is to talk to them calmly and reassuringly until the feeling wears off.

Overdose

Drug overdoses can harm the mind and body, and some can be fatal. It is not thought to be possible to overdose on marijuana. However, small children who take marijuana by mistake (sometimes in the form of a cake or cookie) can end up unconscious. This increases the risk of death, from inhaling vomit while unconscious.

Because the production of marijuana is not controlled, the strength of the drug varies. So, even though users think that they are taking the same amount of drug as normal, they can easily take a stronger dose. This can result in a fast heartbeat and feelings of extreme anxiety and fear. The best treatment for this is calm reassurance while the person waits for his or her body to break down the chemicals that are causing the unpleasant sensation.

Sleepiness

Early in the 20th century, anti-drug activists said that marijuana made people aggressive and contributed to violent crime. In fact, the opposite appears to be true. Marijuana tends to produce tranquillity and sleepiness, which are far removed from the activity required to be aggressive.

The sleepiness caused by marijuana definitely affects the user's ability to operate machinery safely, to ride a bike, or to drive. Marijuana reduces the ability to concentrate and to control fine movements and make fine adjustments. It also affects the perception of time and space. It is clearly very dangerous for someone to drive or to operate other machinery when they have used marijuana.

A menace on the roads

"Marijuana is a menace on the roads. It disrupts drivers' ability to finely control movement and they become dangerous. At present we can't test for being high at the roadside, but we are working on tests. If we suspect that someone is under the influence of a narcotic substance, then we take them to the police station for further tests. The penalties for being intoxicated while in control of a car are severe, with good reason. When you are driving, you are in charge of a powerful machine that is capable of killing innocent people if it is not handled carefully. Imagine how you would feel if someone you love was killed by a driver who was high. People have to take responsibility for their actions. You should never drive if you have taken anything that may affect your judgment, concentration, or ability to control a vehicle."
(Alex, police officer)

Marijuana and addiction

Whether marijuana is addictive or not is debatable. For a drug to be considered addictive, one or more of the following must be true.

- The drug has to affect the user in such a way that the user continues to use it regularly and repetitively, despite any unpleasant effects it may have on the user's body or life.
- The user has to experience a physical need or a psychological need to use the drug, and the need has to be so strong that the user feels compelled to keep on using the drug.
- The drug has to activate the parts of the brain that are activated by normal pleasures, such as food, sex, or laughing.
- Usually, the drug has to cause unpleasant symptoms for the user when it is no longer used.

Not everyone who uses an addictive drug becomes addicted to it. It depends on many factors, such as genetic makeup, family history, personality, mental health, and general physical health.

It seems that it is possible to become psychologically dependent on marijuana. Some users feel that they come to rely on it to help them cope with life. However, this is nothing like addiction to heroin and cocaine. These drugs take over the brain's ability to experience pleasure and are very powerful. Marijuana does not affect the pleasure areas of the brain and does not seem to produce a physical dependence.

"My sister tried pot at college. Mom was really worried that she would turn into a drug addict and drop out of college. She didn't, though. I think she only tried it once or twice."
(Karen, age 13)

Users of heroin and cocaine require more and more of the drug to experience the same effects. This is called tolerance. The same can happen for marijuana users, but the increase in dose needed to produce an effect is very low and so tolerance to marijuana takes a long time to develop.

3 The Cannabis Plant Today
Providing for Modern Needs

In an effort to prevent people from using the plant as a drug, the cultivation of cannabis was generally banned in the 20th century. However, arguments have always been put forward that the plant can be put to many uses and that it is valuable from an environmental point of view. Cannabis products are renewable (you can grow as much as you need) and biodegradable (they break down harmlessly when disposed of). Over the last part of the 20th century, the laws preventing people from growing cannabis for hemp were gradually relaxed. It is now grown as a legal crop in many countries, for its fiber, its seeds, and its oil.

Cannabis fiber—strong and durable materials

The most useful fiber produced from cannabis is hemp. It comes from the *cannabis sativa* variety of the plant, which grows tall and therefore produces long fibers. Industrial hemp production is now legal across most of Western Europe. Cannabis is also grown as an industrial crop in Canada and in four U.S. states: Hawaii, Minnesota, Vermont, and North Dakota. However, it is uncertain whether the U.S. Drug Enforcement Agency will allow farmers to continue planting the crop. They fear that any relaxation of the laws on growing cannabis will increase the amount used as a drug. They feel that the risk of increasing the use of cannabis as a drug is much greater than the environmental

Traditional use
Strong and durable hemp rope is still used at sea, even though ropes made from new synthetic materials are also available.

Tough threads
Clothing made from hemp fiber has a reputation for being hard-wearing.

and industrial benefits of using cannabis for fiber. Hemp fiber is strong, hard-wearing, and resistant to rotting. It has always been considered the best fiber for making rope and sacking, especially for use in ships and industry. Hemp fiber is also used to make cheap, hard-wearing clothing. Cloth made from hemp is very similar to cotton or linen. It is warm in winter and cool in summer.

Hemp fiber has recently found a new niche in the building industry. It is manufactured into "press board" or "composite board," which is much more durable and elastic than fiberboard made from wood pulp. French scientists have also developed hemp into a material that is used as a filler to insulate the walls of buildings to prevent heat loss and reduce noise pollution.

> "I have a pencil case made from hemp. I didn't realize that hemp was from the same plant as marijuana."
> (Rachael, 6th grader)

Another use of hemp fiber is in making string, paper, packaging, and plastics for items like skateboards and car bodies. The car company DaimlerChrysler was one of the first to experiment with using hemp fibers in the construction of its cars, although they did not proceed because of legal problems with obtaining the fiber. Hemp is now used in the interiors of many Mercedes-Benz cars, and other companies are looking at using hemp components in car bodies, too.

Cannabis fuel

Cannabis stalks contain a lot of fiber and cellulose and these can be converted into fuel in two ways. One process, called pyrolysis, converts the stalks into a substance like charcoal, which can be burned to produce energy. The other process involves fermenting the stalks to produce the chemicals methanol and ethanol, which can be used as a fuel. Hemp seed oil can also be processed into a form of fuel.

Cannabis seeds

Cannabis seeds are commonly used as an animal feed and are popular with birds. They are highly nutritious and, since the seeds from *cannabis sativa* contain hardly any of the intoxicating chemicals associated with cannabis, they are also considered by many to be a good food for humans.

Diesel

The diesel engine was developed with the idea that it would be powered by fuel made from agricultural waste, such as hemp stalks. This did not happen, however, because of the laws against growing cannabis. The engines were converted to use diesel fuel instead.

Traditional recipes

Hemp seeds have a place in many countries' cooking. In Lithuania hemp seeds are traditionally served with herrings. Raw or roasted hemp seeds are a traditional and popular snack in China. Hemp seed oil is used for cooking in the more remote areas of Nepal. In eastern Europe and the Baltic states, hemp was added to soups and stews and traditionally ground into a paste similar to peanut butter, which was eaten with bread. Before it was possible to separate hemp seed from its tough outer casing, this paste was hard and gritty. It is still used in eastern Europe and Russia and in places where it can be bought in food stores.

Hemp seed contains approximately 25 percent protein, 30 percent carbohydrate, and 15 percent fiber. It is a good source of essential fatty acids and it also contains carotene, phosphorous, potassium, magnesium, sulphur, calcium, iron, zinc, and vitamins E, C, B1, B2, B3, and B6. It can be used as an ingredient in cookies, snacks, veggie burgers, and porridge. Hemp seed oil is not suitable for frying, because it does not store well, but it is used in a number of processed foods such as sauces.

"We bought some hemp hand cream for my grandma. She loves gardening and it's supposed to be good for your skin."
(Amy, age 10)

Hemp oil

Hemp oil is reported to be good for the skin and so it is used in many cosmetic products such as hand cream, soap, shampoos, and moisturizing cream. Hemp oil is also used as a lamp oil, in the printing industry, for lubricating industrial machines, in household detergents, and in a similar way to linseed oil in paints, varnishes, resins, and stain removers.

Medical uses of marijuana

The properties of marijuana as a medicine have been recognized throughout history, but 20th-century laws prevented doctors from using it to treat their patients. However, synthetic forms of marijuana have recently come onto the market to treat some illnesses under tightly controlled conditions. The laws governing what can and cannot be prescribed to patients are constantly under review.

Improving the appetite

Marijuana users sometimes talk about "the munchies" to describe the hunger and increased appreciation of food that marijuana gives them. In the past, doctors used marijuana to treat diseases that reduce the appetite and cause profound weight loss. Diseases with that effect today include AIDS and some

Therapeutic or recreational

Therapeutic drugs are drugs prescribed by a medically qualified practitioner, or sold by a pharmacy, in order to cure or relieve the symptoms of an illness or injury.

Recreational drugs are taken by an individual in order to change their mood or their state of mind.

cancers, and some modern doctors would like to be permitted to prescribe marijuana for people with these conditions. They say that cannabis may help sufferers to feel hungry and to enjoy a meal, something that they find very difficult without assistance. Eating is one of our basic needs, and being unable to enjoy food can result not only in weakness and loss of weight but also in depression.

"I have leukemia and the chemotherapy makes me feel very sick. I hate it. Every time I see the hospital now, I throw up. My doctor hasn't found a drug to stop me from feeling so sick yet."
(Boris, age 12)

Reducing nausea

As well as stimulating the appetite, marijuana can reduce nausea (feeling sick). Nausea can be a problem for people undergoing chemotherapy treatment for cancer. Some doctors would like marijuana to be legalized for medical use, in order to help these patients. In the United States, a synthetic form of marijuana, Dronabinol, was licensed for use as an anti-emetic (anti-sickness medicine) in 1985. In Britain, a synthetic equivalent of one of the chemicals in marijuana was licensed in 1982, as long as it was only used for patients for whom nothing else worked, and as long as it did not leave the hospital. Some patients feel that this is unfair, as many of them feel sick before, during, and after chemotherapy.

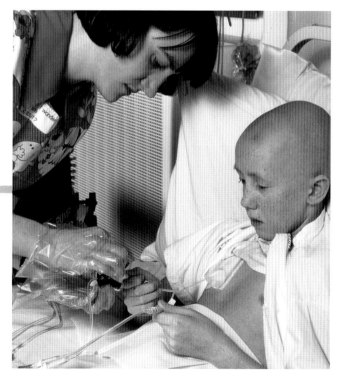

Chemotherapy
The drugs used in chemotherapy are very powerful, in order to control or destroy the cancer cells. The treatment can make the patient feel very sick.

Treating glaucoma

Glaucoma is a condition that affects the eyes. Your eyes are filled with a clear fluid, which helps to keep the eyes' round shape. Small channels allow excess fluid to drain away, so that the pressure within the eye remains steady. In glaucoma, the channels become blocked and the pressure gradually increases, and this affects the eyesight. Eventually the person can become blind. Glaucoma is one of the most common causes of blindness and affects approximately 1.5 percent of 50-year-olds and 5 percent of 70-year-olds.

Treatment for glaucoma is difficult and has unpleasant side effects. Some studies of the effects of smoking marijuana have found that the drug reduces the pressure within the eye, although it is not certain how this works. Pharmaceutical companies are trying to develop an eye-drop that contains marijuana for treating glaucoma.

Taking marijuana for multiple sclerosis

Multiple sclerosis (often known as MS) is a medical condition that disrupts the normal function of the nerves, brain, and spinal cord. The illness comes and goes unpredictably, and attacks can last for weeks or months. Each attack leaves the sufferer with slightly more disability. Because the spinal cord and brain are involved, the attacks can cause symptoms anywhere in the body. These can include tingling, numbness, blurred vision, tiredness, paralysis, muscle cramps, spasms and pain, loss of bladder or bowel control, constipation, and depression. The causes of MS are not yet clearly understood, but it is probably linked to a problem with the immune system.

The muscle spasms, cramps, and pain can be hard to live with and they are difficult to treat. Many of the medicines available have unpleasant side effects and can be addictive if used long term. Marijuana has long been known for its effectiveness at reducing muscle pain, spasms, and cramps. Today, there are many MS sufferers who risk legal prosecution by taking marijuana, because they feel it is the only drug that really relieves their pain.

Some people with MS report that, when they take marijuana, they regain bladder control. Some who are wheelchair bound claim that marijuana relieves their symptoms so much that they can walk unaided. Individual, personal accounts like these, about the way a chemical affects a disease, are called anecdotal evidence and are not considered reliable by scientists. The World Health Organization feels that there is no conclusive evidence that marijuana does help people with MS. Properly set-up scientific studies are needed to discover whether marijuana is really an effective treatment.

The United States government and most Western countries consider marijuana a drug with no medical use. This makes doing scientific studies on its possible uses very difficult or impossible. However, in Britain, permission was given for trials to take place. The first results of these, published in 2003, seemed to show that marijuana can help relieve some of the pain and discomfort associated with MS, but does not cure the condition.

A difficult dilemma

"MS is a terrible condition. It comes and goes, and each time it flares up, it takes more of you away. I spend most of my time in a wheelchair now. I'm too weak to walk far. I get terrible cramps in my legs. On the Internet some people with MS say that smoking pot has really helped them. I'm not sure. It's illegal and I don't want to go to prison. Maybe I'll try it if it gets worse, but then I don't know how to get pot or how to take it. The trouble is, there is so little treatment for MS. Everyone who has it is desperate for a treatment that works."

(Colin, age 45)

Marijuana for pain control

Marijuana has been used for centuries to treat muscular and nerve pain and there is evidence to support its use as a pain reliever, particularly for chronic pain. Pain caused by cancer, for which traditional medicines cause nausea or other unpleasant side effects, may also be relieved by marijuana or synthetic marijuana-based medicines.

Before marijuana was declared illegal, it was used to treat menstrual cramps and also to relieve labor pain, the pain a woman experiences in childbirth. Because the drug is illegal, there has been little scientific study of the effect of marijuana on this form of pain. One main concern is how the drug might affect the baby before it is born.

"My mom gets really bad migraines. Sometimes she is sick for days. She'd never try pot, though. She hates illegal drugs."
(Roberto, age 15)

Migraines

Migraines are severe headaches that can occur with feelings of sickness, vomiting, and blurred vision and can last for hours or days. Migraines are usually brought on by a trigger, such as bright lights, eating certain foods, or hormonal changes. About 20 percent of adults have had a migraine at some point in their lives and many suffer from them frequently. In the 19th century, marijuana was a favorite treatment for migraines.

There has been very little scientific research into the effects of marijuana on migraines. Some doctors and pharmaceutical companies feel that it would be worth carrying out such research to see if marijuana could be an effective treatment.

Migraine misery
One in five adults suffers from migraines.

4 Marijuana and the Law
A "Hot" Topic

Under U.S. law, marijuana is classified as a schedule 1 narcotic. Other drugs in this group include LSD, heroin, and cocaine. Schedule 1 drugs are classified as such because they are highly addictive and of no medical use, and their use is associated with crime and violence. The courts can impose the longest prison sentences for people found to be using, selling, or smuggling these drugs. The United Nations Treaty 406 Single Convention on Narcotic Drugs (1961) aimed to outlaw marijuana production and use around the world by 1991. Although this target was not achieved, the production of marijuana is now illegal in most countries. In Britain marijuana was recently reclassified as Class C schedule 1. This means that it is still illegal to possess marijuana, but people caught only once with a very small amount will not be prosecuted. People found with more than a very small amount will be prosecuted as dealers.

British drug haul

Large quantities of marijuana are illegally trafficked every year. This haul of 20 tons (18 metric tons) was discovered at a British warehouse in 1996.

Many people disagree with marijuana's legal status. Some doctors reject the idea that marijuana has no medical value. Some users argue that it is not a dangerous drug. Manufacturers want to use hemp fiber in industry. There are continuing debates all over the world about whether marijuana should be "declassified." Other people continue to view marijuana as a highly dangerous "gateway" drug.

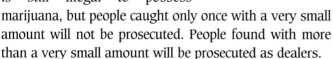

Gateway drugs

People who become addicted to drugs such as heroin or crack cocaine have nearly always used another more socially acceptable, "soft" drug before they were introduced to heroin or cocaine. Common examples of these soft drugs include alcohol, tobacco, marijuana, steroids, and inhalants (glue sniffing). There is a theory that these drugs act as a "gateway" to "hard" drugs. Using a gateway drug does not directly cause someone to go on to try other drugs, but it may introduce them to people who have access to these types of drug. It also introduces them to the behavior associated with drug use, such as deceiving other people about using drugs, and using drugs at specific times. Therefore they may be more likely to try another drug than someone who does not use soft drugs.

Marijuana crimes

Growing cannabis

It is a crime in most countries to grow cannabis or to allow your home to be used for growing cannabis. In many countries a license can be obtained from the government to grow the varieties of cannabis that have very low concentrations of psychoactive chemicals, for fiber, seed, and oil use.

Processing marijuana

It is a crime to process marijuana. This includes harvesting the drug-laden resin from the flower tops or collecting and drying the leaves and seeds, whether it is for personal use or to be sold to other people.

Smuggling and trafficking

It is a crime to import or export marijuana, whether you intend to supply other people or use the drug yourself. People convicted of trafficking drugs tend to receive long prison sentences, since these are considered the most serious types of crime.

● *Supplying and dealing marijuana*

It is a crime to supply marijuana to another person, whether you are paid for it or not.

● *Possessing marijuana*

The possession of marijuana is a crime in most countries, but the penalties in different countries range from cautions to fines to long prison sentences.

During the late 20th century, several U.S. states relaxed their laws on the medical use of marijuana. People with chronic pain or medical conditions that might benefit from treatment with marijuana were therefore able to use the drug without fear of going to prison. Because hemp products such as clothing and cosmetics have also started to gain popularity in the United States there were attempts by some states to restart the growing of cannabis for hemp fiber. However, in 2000 the Drug Enforcement Agency clamped down and is currently trying to stop the sale of any cannabis-based food or cosmetic product.

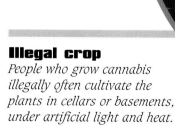

Illegal crop

People who grow cannabis illegally often cultivate the plants in cellars or basements, under artificial light and heat.

Legal use
Customers in certain cafés in Amsterdam are permitted to use small amounts of marijuana.

Different approaches

Some countries have experimented with different ways of managing marijuana use. In 1974 the Netherlands changed its drug laws so that some coffee shops are licensed to sell small amounts of marijuana, under tightly controlled conditions, for use only on their premises. Some people see this project as a success. Recent statistics show that the percentage of young people using marijuana in the Netherlands is smaller than in several other European countries. Other people feel that the availability of marijuana has helped to make the Netherlands a haven for drug smugglers and drug users, although there does not seem to be much evidence to support this opinion.

The laws on the commercial production of cannabis were relaxed in Britain and across much of Europe in the 1980s and a few farmers started small-scale production. Hemp products and cosmetics and foods containing hemp oil are

European statistics

Percentages of people aged 15–34 who had used marijuana in the last 12 months:

Denmark	13.1%
Finland	4.9%
France	17%
Germany	13%
Ireland	17.7%
Netherlands	9.8%
Norway	8.1%
Portugal	6.2%
Spain	12.7%
Sweden	1%
United Kingdom	16.6%

(from a 2002 report)

commonly for sale. In Britain there have been experiments in relaxing the laws for possession of small amounts of marijuana for personal use. It was felt that police were spending too much time arresting and processing people who were found in possession of very small amounts of cannabis for personal use.

In a pilot study in south London, people found with small amounts of marijuana were cautioned rather than being arrested. The study was generally thought to have been successful in retargeting police time to deal with crimes involving drugs like crack cocaine and heroin.

Arguments for legalizing marijuana use

The following are some of the points made by people who argue that marijuana use should be legalized.

- Marijuana is a naturally occurring herb with beneficial properties.
- Marijuana is not physically addictive.
- Marijuana provides a possible medical treatment for several symptoms, diseases, and conditions that are hard to treat using normal medicines. These include muscle spasm in multiple sclerosis, nausea connected with chemotherapy, the wasting associated with AIDS, and the eye condition called glaucoma. People who have painful and disabling diseases and who find marijuana helpful have to commit a crime in order to obtain marijuana for medical use. Many people argue that it is absurd to threaten prison sentences to very sick people who buy marijuana in a desperate attempt to find relief from pain or the wasting associated with some forms of cancer and AIDS.
- Marijuana has been used for thousands of years and the plant has many other practical uses, including for making rope, cloth, paper, fuel for cars, biodegradable plastics, animal feed, cosmetics, detergents, and building materials.

⌐) It is preferable to use marijuana for these products, as they are less damaging to the environment than petroleum-based products. Cannabis is a renewable crop that does not need large amounts of pesticides to grow healthily. Also, many of the products made from cannabis are biodegradable, which means that, when they are thrown away they do not pollute the environment.

⌐) The police time spent on arresting or prosecuting people for possession of marijuana could be used more profitably, for tracking down the people who profit the most from illegal drug use and who are responsible for selling drugs to the most vulnerable.

⌐) Marijuana is attractive to young users because it is illegal. Controlling the use and sale of marijuana and legalizing it will make using it less attractive.

⌐) In the Netherlands where the use of cannabis is legal in well-regulated environments, less than 1 percent of those who try marijuana go on to become problem drug users.

"Marijuana is not like the other drugs, heroin or cocaine. It's never killed anyone. I think we should be allowed to make up our own minds. If you're old enough to smoke tobacco, why shouldn't you be allowed to smoke pot?" (Elsie, age 18)

⌐) Marijuana is much less harmful and much less addictive than many legal drugs, including alcohol and tobacco.

⌐) Cannabis grown for hemp could provide needed income to states and people that currently depend on growing tobacco for income.

Arguments against legalizing marijuana use

People who argue that marijuana use should remain illegal make the following points:

⌐) Not all naturally occurring herbs are beneficial. For example, tobacco and deadly nightshade are herbs but they are toxic. While marijuana is not as toxic as these, it does have some negative effects on health. Smoking marijuana mixed with tobacco puts you at risk of developing lung, throat, and mouth cancers and there is some evidence that taking marijuana puts you at risk of developing mental health problems and heart disease.

- Marijuana users can become psychologically dependent on the drug.

- The medical uses of marijuana have not yet been fully researched, so officially, the jury is still out on whether or not it is a safe and reliable treatment.

- The fact that a drug is a medicine does not mean that it is safe for everyone to use. For example, heroin is used medically to treat severe pain, but it is highly addictive.

- There are two main species of cannabis plant. *Cannabis sativa* grows very tall, producing long fibers suitable for

"I think we should downgrade marijuana. So much of our time is spent dealing with people found in possession of a small amount for personal use. It's time that could be better spent going after the big boys."
(Simon, police officer)

Protests
In many countries people have such strong opinions about marijuana that they take part in protests to try to change the law about the drug.

cloth, rope, and papermaking. It is farmed in many parts of the world and this is acceptable, since it contains only low concentrations of the chemicals that make cannabis psychoactive. To obtain hemp fiber, there is no need to grow *cannabis indica*, the type of the plant that is used for its psychoactive properties. Some people feel that it is unacceptable even to allow the cultivation of *cannabis sativa*. They feel that allowing products made from hemp fiber or oil onto the general market gives people the idea that marijuana is acceptable; and they argue that, therefore, all cannabis products should be banned.

- It is misleading to talk about marijuana as a "soft" drug that is less harmful than "hard" drugs like heroin and cocaine. People making this point argue that there is no real difference between hard and soft drugs; every intoxicating drug has the potential to cause harm, both to the individual using it and to society as a whole.

- If marijuana is legalized, the people who used to try it because it was risky and illegal will move on to the more dangerous drugs that are still illegal, in order still to be daring, and to make money.

"I am strongly against the legalization of marijuana. As far as I'm concerned, there is no such thing as a harmless drug. They all lead people into a life of crime and misery."
(Stella, police officer)

- The United Nations feels that reclassifying marijuana sends the wrong message to people growing·the crop in other countries and puts at risk the worldwide effort to reduce the production of illegal drugs.

- Unlike alcohol, there are currently no roadside tests to indicate if a driver is high on marijuana. This means that people would be more likely to drive high.

- If marijuana is legal it will be easier for children to obtain it.

- Legalizing marijuana would probably cause a big rise in its use and therefore a big increase in the amount of money spent on health care to deal with diseases associated with smoking it.

- Legalizing marijuana could start a trend toward making other, more harmful drugs socially acceptable.

- Marijuana use is immoral. Just because other immoral drugs like tobacco and alcohol are legal doesn't mean that marijuana should be legal, too.

"I don't think they should legalize marijuana. I see drug addicts coming in here every day, up to no good, stealing. They need to be locked up, not left on the street."
(Jim, small business owner)

The arguments about marijuana continue around the world. In the next chapter we investigate who uses marijuana and its impact on today's society.

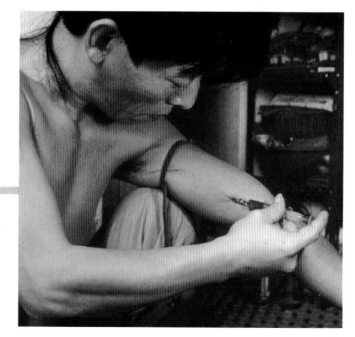

Road to addiction
Some people argue that people who take marijuana are more likely than others to go on to try more dangerous drugs, such as heroin.

5 Marijuana in Society
Considering Your Viewpoint

Marijuana is used by such a diverse section of society that it is impossible to characterize a typical user. Many people first come across marijuana when they are in their late teens or early twenties. It is estimated that, in some parts of the world, well over 20 percent of adults will try marijuana at some point. Of these, only a small fraction will continue to use marijuana regularly, and it is estimated that less than 1 percent go on to try more dangerous drugs such as heroin.

Since World War II, marijuana use has grown consistently, whereas other drugs have gone in and out of fashion. There are several reasons for the increase in marijuana use. People have become richer and so have more money to spend on nonessential things. Many people see marijuana as a less risky illegal drug than others. Third, marijuana is increasingly available.

All types
Statistically, one of these five teenagers will try marijuana at some time in their life.

"I don't want to use marijuana. I like to stay in control of my body."
(Danny, age 15)

The power of public opinion

Many countries around the world are introducing legislation to decriminalize the possession of small amounts of marijuana. One of the reasons for this change is that large sections of the public are in favor of such a move.

Sweden has been one of the most successful European countries at limiting the rise in marijuana use. The European Union estimates that under 8 percent of adults in Sweden have tried marijuana. Sweden has harsh legal penalties for the possession of marijuana and, unlike in other countries, a person in Sweden can be prosecuted if the police think that they may have used marijuana, even if no drugs are found on the person. However, the success of the anti-marijuana campaign in Sweden is not only due to its penalties. Sweden has a long history of public intolerance for the use of any intoxicating substance, including alcohol and tobacco. Swedish public opinion is very much against the use of any recreational drug, legal or otherwise, and so very few people there want to buy marijuana.

Other people suggest that Sweden's success is because it borders countries that have a more tolerant approach to recreational drugs, so that anyone wishing to get drunk or "stoned" (high) crosses the border into Denmark or Norway.

Cannabis and the environment

The campaign for the legalization of cannabis growing and marijuana is often associated with environmentalists. They emphasize the need to

Drug use

Countries around the world have united to try to reduce illegal drug use and drug crime, and their efforts have been fairly successful. The numbers of people taking drugs that are obviously very risky, like cocaine and heroin, are stable (not going up) or declining.

"In Sweden we don't like drugs. They are not good for the body or the mind."
(Goren, age 15)

prevent pollution and waste and to ensure that the earth continues to be able to sustain life. Environmental pressure groups support the legalization of marijuana mainly because the cannabis plant has multiple uses. The activists point out that growing cannabis for hemp fiber and oil would help solve some of today's environmental problems. For example, using hemp fiber to make fiberboard, building materials, and even car bodies has an important advantage: Cannabis is considered a "carbon dioxide neutral" plant.

Carbon dioxide is produced by most industrial processes that involve burning fuel. It is one of the pollutants known as greenhouse gases, which are thought to build up in the atmosphere and contribute to global warming. The processes needed to turn hemp fiber into fiberboard, plastic, or paint produce carbon dioxide; but this is balanced (or "neutralized") by the fact that, while the cannabis plants are growing, they absorb lots of carbon dioxide from the air and give out

Air pollution
Waste gases from industry pollute the air, whether the industry uses petrochemicals or hemp fiber. But growing more hemp to use in industry could help reduce air pollution.

Global warming and greenhouse gases

Global warming is a term used by scientists to refer to increases in temperature on the earth, caused by the effect of "greenhouse gases." Global warming may lead to changes in rainfall patterns around the world, a rise in sea levels, and a change to the climate that would affect plant and animal life.

Greenhouse gases are gases present in the earth's atmosphere that trap heat from the sun. Without these gases (which include water vapor, carbon dioxide, nitrous oxide, and methane), the earth would be very cold. The concern is that human activity is producing so much of these gases that we are in danger of making the earth warmer than it would naturally be. Even a small rise in the average temperature of the earth can cause problems for humans, animals, and plants.

oxygen, through photosynthesis. Taking this into account, using hemp fiber in industrial processes is said to produce less carbon dioxide than using petrochemicals. Growing more cannabis, in order to use hemp fiber rather than petrochemicals in more industrial processes, could therefore reduce the greenhouse gases in the atmosphere.

Cannabis fiber is considered "environmentally friendly" in other ways, too. For example, cloth made from hemp looks and feels very similar to cotton, but growing a crop of cannabis requires far fewer pesticides than growing cotton plants. Therefore, people argue that using hemp fiber rather than cotton for making cloth would reduce the usage of poisonous chemical pesticides, which are dangerous to animals and humans and which pollute the environment. Also, cannabis plants can be grown at a much higher density than cotton plants, and this means that more fiber can be produced on less land. This, as well as the smaller amount of pesticides needed, makes hemp fiber cheaper to produce than cotton.

What is your attitude?

It is possible that some people you know may use marijuana and that you may be invited to try it. It is a good idea to prepare yourself in advance for situations where you may encounter marijuana. If someone offered you a joint, what would you do? Are you fully aware of the risks? Do you know what it is you are being offered? What is the best way to say "no"? Practicing saying no in different situations is called role playing. It is usually better if you can role play with a friend, so you can discuss different ways of handling a situation. As you think about your attitude toward marijuana as a drug, you need to be fully aware of the risks.

The risks involved in taking marijuana

- You can never be sure exactly what you are taking. Some drug dealers mix or "bulk up" the drugs they sell with other, less valuable substances in order to increase their profit. Although marijuana is less easy than other drugs to adulterate in this way, the possibility is still there. The unknown substances mixed with the marijuana could be dangerous.

- You do not know the concentration of chemicals in marijuana, so you can never be sure of what the effects will be. High-grade marijuana can cause severe anxiety and can be very unpleasant.

- You may cause an accident if you try to drive a car or ride a bike under the influence of marijuana.

What would you do?

If you found yourself in a situation where people were smoking pot, what would you do? Knowing about the drug and all its risks will help you make your decision with confidence.

Expelled

"My brother was expelled from school. There were undercover cops at a teen club he was at and they caught him buying some pot from a dealer they were watching. It was really bad. Mom and Dad went ballistic. Mom wouldn't stop crying, saying that he had ruined the family's good name. He was about to take his SATs, too. He was just trying to show off in front of his girlfriend, but she wasn't impressed when he was arrested. Because he was expelled, Mom and Dad had to find him another school. I think he's going to be grounded for the rest of his life."
(Sophie, age 15)

- Mixing drugs, or taking a drug when you are already under the influence of another, is very dangerous. It is especially dangerous to take any drug at the same time as you are drinking alcohol or taking cold medicine.

- There is a real risk of being caught by the police. You may be arrested and prosecuted. This can have a very bad effect on your future job prospects.

- You run the risk of developing lung disease if you smoke marijuana regularly.

- There is a real risk to other members of your family. Your parents may be arrested and charged if drugs are found in their home.

- You risk being expelled or suspended from school.

- You run the risk of becoming psychologically dependent.

- Marijuana can make you so "laid back" that you stop being bothered by anything. Although this may seem like a good thing, it can mean that you stop making the effort to have good relationships with the people who are important to you, and that you stop trying to succeed at school or work. Therefore it can have a very damaging effect on your future career and family life.

"There's too many things to do to waste time taking drugs. I want to be in there making things happen, not asleep."
(Cameron, age 14)

Glossary

addiction   when people need a drug in order to relieve unpleasant symptoms experienced when they stop taking it. This happens because the body has adapted to the drug being present, so when it is not present, the body craves it.

addictive   causing addiction

bong   pipe used for smoking marijuana

chronic   lasting a long time. Chronic pain is pain that lasts for more than a few months.

craving   desperate and urgent longing

dependence   physical dependence on a drug is a condition in which if the person suddenly stops taking the drug, his or her body reacts badly and the person feels sick. Psychological dependence occurs when the person feels a strong need to take the drug, which is not related to any physical changes in the body.

drug   chemical that is taken into the body in order to change the person's physical or mental state

endorphins   pain-relieving chemicals that are produced naturally in the brain

fibers   fine thread-like strands that can be of animal, plant, or humanmade origin. Many fibers are twisted or woven together to produce materials like sewing thread, rope, string, or cloth.

flowering tops   the flower parts of a plant

glaucoma   condition in which the pressure within the eye increases. This can result in sight defects and eventually blindness.

hallucinogenic   causing the perception of something that is not really there (a hallucination). This can involve seeing, hearing, smelling, tasting, or feeling.

hemp   fibers produced from the cannabis plant, which can be processed into materials such as cloth, rope, or building materials. Sometimes people refer to the cannabis plant as a hemp plant and sometimes the word "hemp" is used to refer to the less psychoactive variety of cannabis that is often grown for its fiber, oil, and seeds.

high   slang for the experience of being under the influence of a psychoactive drug

hormones   group of chemical messengers produced by glands or organs in the body and that affect other parts of the body. For example, the hormone progesterone is produced during the female menstrual cycle and prepares a woman's body to become pregnant.

immune system   system in the body that protects it from infection

inhale   to breathe in. People who smoke marijuana inhale the smoke in order to become intoxicated.

insulate   to prevent heat, cold, or electricity from passing from one side of a barrier to another. People insulate their homes to prevent heat from escaping during the winter.

intoxicant   something that makes you feel drunk, excited, and/or elated

intoxicating   causing the experience of being drunk, excited, and/or elated

munchies	slang term for the hunger people feel after they have smoked marijuana
narcotic	drug that affects the brain to produce dizziness, euphoria, sleepiness, and may eventually cause unconciousness and death
nausea	feeling that you may be going to vomit (throw up)
neuro-transmitters	chemicals that carry a message across a junction (synapse) between two nerves. Neurotransmitters are mainly found in the brain and spinal cord.
opiates	drugs made from the opium poppy. These include morphine, codeine, opium, and heroin.
overdose	taking too much of a drug. This usually causes physical or mental damage.
pesticides	chemicals used to kill insects that eat and destroy crops
psychoactive	affecting the brain and behavior
recreational	leisure-time. Recreational drugs are drugs used to achieve a "high" rather than for any medical reason.
resin	sticky substance produced in the sap of some plants and trees

selectively bred	genetically engineered by selecting plants or animals that display a certain desirable quality and breeding only from them until a variety of plant or animal is produced that always exhibits the quality required
therapeutic	having to do with healing the body or mind
tolerance	ability to endure something without showing serious effects. If the body is regularly exposed to a particular drug, it may become tolerant to it. This means that the body learns to react to minimize the effects of the drug and so the user needs to take an increased dose of the drug to get the same effects.
trafficking	illegal trading in a drug or smuggling a drug into a country
withdrawal	process the body goes through when a person stops taking a drug

Resources

Further Reading

Connolly, Sean. *Marijuana*. Chicago: Heinemann, 2003.

Lawler, Jennifer. *Drug Legalization: A Pro/Con Issue*. Berkeley Heights, N.J.: Enslow Publishers, 2000.

Westcott, Patty. *Why Do People Take Drugs?* Chicago: Raintree, 2001.

Organizations

Child Welfare League of America
440 First Street NW
Washington, DC 20001
(202) 638-2952
www.cwla.org

D.A.R.E. America
P.O. Box 775
Dumfries, VA 22026
(703) 860-3273
www.dare.com

Marijuana Anonymous
www.marijuana-anonymous.org

Partnership for a Drug Free America
405 Lexington Avenue, Suite 1601
New York, NY 10174
(212) 922-1560
www.drugfreeamerica.org

Index